THE

CHURCH...

A HOSPITAL?

By

PROLIFIC, INTERNATIONAL BESTSELLING
AUTHOR

JOHN A. ANDREWS

AUTHOR OF

THE 5 STEPS TO CHANGING YOUR LIFE

THE 5 Ps FOR TEENS

QUOTES UNLIMITED

DARE TO MAKE A DIFFERENCE-SUCCESS 101

SPREAD SOME LOVE - RELATIONSHIPS 101

&

TOTAL COMMITMENT-THE MINDSET OF
CHAMPIONS

THE CHURCH...A HOSPITAL?

Books That Will Enhance Your Life

A L I
Andrews Leadership International
                    www.ALI Pictures.com
                    www.JohnAAndrews.com

ISBN: **978-1540861627**
Cover Design: ALI
Front Cover Deign: ALI
Edited by: ALI

THE CHURCH… A HOSPITAL?

TABLE OF CONTENTS

THE CHURCH...A HOSPITAL?

This book is dedicated to my mother, Elaine Louisa Andrews, who not only planted in me an appetite for God's word but lived a life of dedication and service to her church and community. Also to my sons Jonathan, Jefferri, and Jamison, who keep me filled with passion, persistence and purpose.

We Spend Much Of Our Time Learning About Going To Heaven, And Forget About Having A Little Heaven Down Here ... Before We Get There.

JOHN A. ANDREWS

CHAPTER 1

The Church, prepared as a bride to meet Jesus (its bridegroom) is sometimes labeled as both a physical and spiritual institution. Inside are housed the fallen, sick, broken spirited and confused human beings as well as those who are/or striving to be spiritually healthy and cherish a genuine relationship with the same Jesus.

THE CHURCH...A HOSPITAL?

IMAGINE IF YOU WERE STRICKEN with cancer, and as your physician, I were to tell you that the cure for your almost fatal disease lies beneath the river bed. What if I prescribed that if you found, a little smooth rock, glittering as a diamond, placed it twice a day outside the cancer infected area for one month, and you would be cured? What time would you wake up in the morning and what time would you arrive at the river bed?

As you look in the water, noticing several stones ruggedly, smoothly shaped, would you use a net or your bare hands, so you can feel the contour and identify of your cure easily?

In order to ensure your success and beat the odds, let's say you decided to use your hands. If sunset came and you didn't find it, now with blistered hands, would you return the following day to continue your search? By now you have cleared almost all the stones from that river bed, but that special stone was yet to be found. Not only are your hands aching and bloodied, but your back hurts severely. The sun sets again. You drag yourself home.

Now furious about the price you have paid thus far, you pick up the phone and call me complaining, "Where is that stone? I've looked all over; I'm sore. It's nowhere to be found." And I respond, "Keep looking, the stone is there, plus you need to start medicating tomorrow."

Now you jump out of bed before the crack of dawn, so

you can get to that river bed, fearing that a high tide of water will wash your medication away.

Then right before sunset, with what little energy you have left, you clear more rocks from that river bed. Just when you were about to give up, you discovered the smooth stone - the cure for your disease.

Knowing that you have a whole month of treatment to go, you feel as though you've already been cured. You call me back jubilantly. Forgetting the pain you've gone through, you shout out, "I've found it, I've found it! I love you, doctor. Thanks for saving my life." I respond, "What a thrill of success. You committed to the process and now you have success. YES! "

AS A MEMBER OF THE SPIRITUAL realm objective beckons - spiritual health. Athletes are known to exercise daily in order to maintain a healthy and fit body. They are also known to leave it all on the field or court in order to produce a victory. Writers and I can testify to this: are known to write consistently in order to hone their craft. Additionally, whenever a writer's block occurs they rely on certainly proven exercises which aid in getting them back on track. Doctors and lawyers, classified as two of the most prestigious occupations in our world today thrive on continuing education not only to maintain their educational status but to be a notch above the rest in their profession. Actors, including mega stars, retain a coach who can assist them in mastering their craft. Birds migrate out of their free will in order to escape the cold climate and embrace the warmth. Squirrels gather their nuts in the fall in order to have a full supply of food during the cold winter months. Yet we (human beings), created a little lower than the angels struggle consistently to become healthy.

Are you willing to do what it takes in order to establish a genuine relationship with the Great Physician and become spiritually healthy? What if Jesus was ready to heal you and his voice beckoned this very moment?

CHAPTER 2

Today, around the world, throughout numerous health institutions many with broken bodies as well as broken minds congregate. Some have been stricken with devastating external bodily ailments such as birth defects, skin cancer, epilepsy, Parkinson's disease and broken limbs. While others suffer terminally and internally with cancer, HIV Aids, diabetes, lupus, and lymphoma, to name a few.

On the other hand, the Church, designed to be a place to make people pious and well-behaved has become the residence for individuals with broken spirits, broken relationships, strokes, demons, shipwrecked aspirations, and emptiness.

Not to mention those affected with sins of the body: fornication, adultery, and sticky fingers. Additionally, those stricken with the sins of the mind or the heart such as lust, hypocrisy, covetousness, blasphemy, malice, envy, strife, pride, jealousy, bigotry, witchcraft, as well as un-forgiveness.

In Proverbs 4:23 we are admonished: "Watch over your heart with diligence, for from it flows the spring of life." How one thinks has a tremendous effect on what transpires. Nothing is more damaging than sins of the heart or mind, mainly because they are secretive and cannot be contained within the heart.

Proverbs 23:7 echoes, "For as a man thinketh within himself, so he is." A truism also states: "Input equals output."

Sins of the mind, those surreptitious sins of the heart dates back to the first murderer – Cain. In those early days, Cain killed his brother Abel mainly out of jealousy. It was said: Abel offered up a better sacrifice than Cain did. As a result, Cain sought Abel out and took his life.

THE CHURCH...A HOSPITAL?

Humanity has been marching on the road of passions confusion and sin since the fall of the first man – Adam. The Church has become preoccupied with the ultimate fate of human beings since that fall.

Jesus came and gave his life for us; so we might have life and have it abundantly. It is said: "A smart man learns from his mistakes, but a truly wise man learns from the mistakes of others?" It was not his desire for us to live as the Pharisees, Sadducees, and scribes of his time. His numerous parables and healings should suffice.

Yet, we struggle severely in order to measure up. It was clear in the life he lived as he walked on earth: He not only healed the sick, replaced a severed ear, cast out demons, calmed the angry sea, fed the multitudes, mend the broken hearted and raised the dead, as in the case of Lazarus who had been dead for four days and no doubt, was a rancid stench by then. It was said: Lazarus was sick. Jesus was summoned.

However, he didn't come in time to heal him. As a result, Lazarus died. Jesus went to the grave of Lazarus four days later and told the mourners to remove the stone. How it must have shocked them hearing such a statement. Martha, the brother of Lazarus blurted out: "Lord, by this time he stinketh. He had been dead for four days. However, he was four days late. Yet Jesus ignored Martha's concern and said with a loud voice, "Lazarus come forth."

The mourners in total disbelief were stunned as: "bound hand and foot with wrappings, on his face, wrapped with a cloth," Lazarus came forth.

Then Jesus said: "Loose him, and let him go." Lazarus offers us, in my opinion, a graphic illustration of our predicament as regenerate Christians.

CHAPTER 3

The Church, created purely for those who must prepare themselves in order to spend eternity with Jesus Christ when he returns, is also labeled as I mentioned earlier, a therapeutic pathway for the fallen, sick, and confused human beings, and not solely for those who want to walk with Jesus.

THE CHURCH…A HOSPITAL?

Many only embrace Churches whenever major catastrophe hits. Immediately after 911 which terrified New York City with such velocity, and causing thousands to lose their lives. Churches in New York City became overcrowded during subsequent weeks. It's apparent, most people in that city wanted to not only know who Jesus is but if there was another incident as catastrophic as this, would they be ready to meet him in the end. There was none. Neither did He return as many so called prophets claimed he would right afterward.

I resided in Los Angeles California when that incident struck the Big Apple. As a matter of fact, when the second plane slammed into the Twin Towers, it was all seen on my TV.

Months later, I visited New York City and saw a big change in terms of the harsh attitude which many in that city previously exhibited. Their attitudes were softer and Christian-like.

Now, that incident is like water under the bridge, and the site *911 Memorial* stands as a monument for tourists. Most churches have returned to their heathenistic ways and experience a half empty status since that water subsided.

In life, many wait until there's a crisis or being stricken with a serious ailment before they come swinging the Church doors open. Some in the case of paralytics need the assistance of others in order to attend – someone to wheel them in. While some show up only when stricken by a brain stroke.

God, through his miraculous work of creation, created man in his own image on the sixth day after which he rested on the next. The huge responsibility is ours to keep that image intact both in the body as well as in mind. "Create within me a clean heart, O God, and renew within me a right spirit within me," cried David in Psalms 51:10. A story worth recounting.

In The Church...A Hospital? I'll introduce you to doctors, nurses, sick-people, recovering patients, paralytics, those stricken with sins of the mind, dull-minded, egotists, fault finders, and very sick people.

Don't be surprised to find some, who, residing within these pages. Mainly, those who are both mentally and spiritually dead like most of the multitudes which followed Jesus during his tenure here on earth, and seated right next to you and me.

CHAPTER 4

Jesus, while traveling along the border of Samaria and Galilee, came into this village and met a group of people suffering from leprosy. They stood at a distance and called out in a loud voice, "Jesus, Master, have pity on us!" Jesus had compassion on them and said: "Go, show yourselves to the priests," They journeyed and were cleansed. It is a known fact if one were to touch a leper, he or she stands the risk of contracting leprosy. No wonder they cried out: *have pity on us*! It is evident no one came near or dared to associate themselves with them.

One of them, a Samaritan, when he realized he was cleansed of this incurable variety of skin diseases, he returned, threw himself at Jesus' feet and thanked him. Jesus asked, Were not all ten cleansed? Where are the other nine? Has no one returned to give praise except this foreigner?"(Luke 17:17-18 NIV). The cleansed leper, no doubt, lingered at Jesus' feet; in penitence realizing his allies who he must have hung out with for years, refused to show gratitude to the one who had cured them, by at least saying *Thanks*. However, Jesus said to him, "Rise up and go; your faith has made you well." (Luke 17:19 NIV). How the once a "leper" and now cleansed must have leaped for joy.

ONE DAY, Jesus and his disciples, while departing from Bethany, he saw a fig tree in the distance. The tree (as the story was told in the Gospels of Matthew and Mark) had leaves on it, plus Jesus was hungry. So he went to see if the tree had any fruit on it. When he got there, he found nothing but leaves on it. Naturally, it was not the season for figs. Jesus then said to the tree, "May no one ever eat from you again," His disciples, present, heard it. This was yet another in Jesus' repertoire of 40 miracles.

In the morning as they continued their journey, they saw the fig tree withered from its roots. Peter, not forgetting yesterday's miraculous encounter, said to Jesus, "Rabbi, look! The tree you cursed has withered!"

"Have faith in God," Jesus answered. "Truly I tell you, if anyone says to this mountain, 'Go, throw yourself into the sea,' and does not doubt in your heart but believe what they say will happen, it will be done to them.

Therefore I tell you, whatever you ask for in prayer, believe that you have received it, and it will be yours. And when you stand praying, if you hold anything against anyone, forgive them, so that your Father in heaven may forgive you your sins." (Mark 11:12-14; 20-25 NIV).

Forgiveness is a very prominent theme in the Bible. If you include words like *forgive* and *forgiven* and similar derivatives it occurs 116 times. In the Lord's Prayer, the noun *forgive* is found twice along with the noun **kingdom**.

Forgiveness, no doubt is a prerequisite for entering into God's kingdom. If we aren't willing to forgive others, why do we think our heavenly Father would forgive us when we sin. Whenever we choose not to forgive one another, it's like refusing to free ourselves from that vice which the one who has wronged us is also tightly squeezed into.

It might be alarming to know that many adults go to their graves holding onto un-forgiveness from since they were of childhood years. They refuse to live a life free from the guilt of un-forgiveness. Therefore, content with carrying the onus of not forgiving they die in resentfulness and misery.

The Lord's Prayer

Our Father who art in heaven, hallowed be thy name. Thy kingdom come. Thy will be done on earth as it is in heaven. Give us this day our daily bread, and forgive us our trespasses, as we forgive those who trespass against us, and lead us not into temptation, but deliver us from evil.

For thine is the kingdom, and the power, and the glory, for ever and ever.

Amen.

CHAPTER **5**

During Jesus' tenure here on earth, the scribes and Pharisees among others were notorious for tempting and testing his alignment with God. It seems as if his cleansing power and actions were always on trial. They pressured him on everything: including what was lawful to do on the

THE CHURCH...A HOSPITAL?

Sabbath day, who had access to Heaven, who he should dine with, the powers he possessed, the Law of Moses, the authenticity of his miracles, whose Son was he and much more.

One day, they brought unto him a woman taken in adultery, and sat her down in his midst. "They said unto him, Master, this woman was taken in adultery, in the very act. Now the law of Moses counseled that such should be stoned: but what sayest thou?" (John 8:3-4).

It was clear to Jesus they were once again tempting him as they had done on numerous occasions. It was apparent some of them if not all of them were involved in an adulterous act with the woman. Now, they were even referring to her as "such."

Jesus, the master at human relations didn't at this point clear his throat but stooped down, and with his finger wrote on the ground, pretending he hadn't heard them. His actions must have ticked them off. Plus, it seemed at first his message wasn't vividly clear to them. So they pressed him with the rhetorical question. *Now the law of Moses counseled that such should be stoned: but what sayest thou?* In other words, they were demanding an immediate answer while probably eyeing some stones in the vicinity preparatory to stoning her.

On the other hand, Jesus *milked* the process in order to drive home his message. Not only did they see their sins etched in the dirt by Jesus, It was said: "...he lifted up himself, and said unto them, he that is without sin let him cast the first stone at her,"(John 8:7). Ouch! Then he left them *hanging out to dry.*

Once again, he stooped down and wrote on the ground. By this time his message was taking deep root inside their minds as their names were once again etched in the dirt and associated with their sins. Yes, casting the first stone became problematic for the woman's accusers.

"And they which heard it, being convicted by their own conscience, went out one by one, beginning at the eldest, even to the last: and Jesus was left alone, and the woman in the midst.

When Jesus had lifted up himself and saw none but the woman he said unto her, Woman where are thine accusers? Hath no man condemned thee?" (John 8:9-10).

The woman at this point, no doubt was recovering from her guilt mixed with trepidation. She responded: "… No man, Lord.

And Jesus said unto her, Neither do I condemn thee: go, and sin no more," (John 8:11).

Jesus did not only send the woman away but cautioned her to *go and sin no more.*

Her accusers, on the other hand, pricked by their conscience, rejected mentally the cleansing power of Jesus. They opted to remain spiritually dead and fled.

THE CHURCH...A HOSPITAL?

On the other hand, the woman, the accused, and who they referred to as *such* was enjoying the newness of life.

Meanwhile, her accusers were embarrassed, fled and worse of all held onto their sinful ways.

CHAPTER 6

Jesus' related a parable about the sower and the four types of soil. Out of his 46 parables, this one stands out not only in the minds of his disciples back then but also in minds of the multitudes gathered, past and present revelators, as well as biblical scholars of today. A scholastic which includes you and I now that you've been perusing through these pages. Particularly, this parable, it's so relatable to us now living in the end times.

By now I hope it's understood that the purpose of a parable is to cover the real meaning behind the story so that only those who are capable of understanding it or willing to put forth enough effort to find meaning will do so. That effort or ability is where the rubber meets the road in that person's zeal to being educated and developing what some may call a spiritual backbone; necessary to withstand persecution.

It was told: Jesus went out of a house and sat by the sea and great multitudes pressed him. He got into a boat and sat down while they stood on the shore. It was then, he spoke many things in parables, saying: "Behold, a sower went out to sow," (Matthew 13:3). Jesus realizing their minds were cluttered, worked on taking their minds away from the house, the dirt yard, the backyard and had them present at the seashore, watching the waves roll in, in order to allegorically address them in farming terminologies.

Jesus continued: "And as he sowed, some seed fell by the wayside; and the birds devoured them. Some fell on stony places, where they did not have much earth; they immediately sprang up because they had no depth of earth. But when the sun was up they were scorched, and because they had no root they withered away.

THE CHURCH...A HOSPITAL?

And some fell among thorns, and thorns sprang up and choked them. But others fell on good ground and yielded a crop, some a hundredfold, some sixty, some thirty. He who has ears to hear, let him hear."

Now his disciples must have seen their confused looks evolve since Jesus departed from the house and they began to follow, plus as he launched into the telling of this parable. The disciples asked: "...Why do you speak to them in parables?"

He answered and said unto them, "Because it had been given unto you to know the mysteries of the kingdom of heaven, but to them it has not been given. For whosoever has, to him more will be given, and he will have abundance; but whoever does not have, even what he has will be taken away from him." (Matthew 13:4-12).

Jesus further explained that the method to his speaking in parables was because the hearts of these people had grown dull. Additionally, *their ears are hard of hearing, and their eyes have closed, lest they should see with their eyes and hear with their ears, lest they should understand with their hearts and turn so that **He would heal them**.* Verse 16. Some of these people no doubt had been listening to Jesus preaching and teaching for years. They had seen his numerous miracles. It is said: *Seeing is believing.* Yet many did not believe. Many had hardened their hearts. Many had accused him of Satanic works and rejected His word.

THE CHURCH...A HOSPITAL?

Jesus also took this opportunity to ensure his disciples understood on a higher level: the sowing strategy as well as the functions of the soil. Additionally, he wanted his disciples to: not take what he disclosed in this parable for granted as the multitudes did. His disciples had been so close to him. They had seen and experienced his miraculous works, and even on a spiritual level much unlike others, especially in the case of Peter, James, and John. It was important to Jesus that they understood what he had been trying to convey to them all along. *He didn't want them to miss the boat.*

Jesus continued: "Therefore, hear the parable of the sower: When anyone hears the word of the kingdom, and does not understand it, then the wicked one comes and snatch away what was sown in his heart. This is he who received the seed by the wayside.

But he who received the seeds on stony places, this is he who hears the word and immediately receives it with joy; yet he has no root in himself, but endures only for a while. For then when tribulation or persecution arises because of the word, immediately he stumbles.

Now he who received seed among the thorns is he who hears the word, and the cares of this world and the deceitfulness of riches choke the word and he becomes unfruitful.

But he who received the seed on good ground is he who hears the word and understands it, who indeed bears fruit and produces: some a hundredfold, some sixty, some thirty." (Matthew 13:18-23).

We find this parable is on the ground more than on the sower himself. This sower went out to the field to sow some seed, he scattered them and the seeds fell where they must – on all different kinds of ground.

The seeds which fell on good ground, we should note, they produced different yields. Also, the same seed scattered from the hands of the sower, some produced no crop, some crop or even a great crop.

It needs restating: *He who has ears, let him hear.* Not everyone is willing to listen, and even those who listen they too listen on different levels.

Sometimes it takes more than reading and hearing to understand God's word. Revelation in many cases is necessary. A classic example can be seen in the life and works of Ellen G. White and others. Also, it is necessary for the spirit to open our eyes as well as our hearts in order for us to understand.

Before we launch into the reality of our modern day story, let's dive a little deeper as we uncover some additional noteworthy characters.

CHAPTER 7

Joseph was sold into slavery by his begrudging, cruel and deceitful brothers. When he arrived in Egypt, he was sold to a very powerful man, Potiphar. Joseph worked his way up through Potiphar's ranks and put in charge of everything in Potiphar's household except his wife. Joseph by now had forgiven his brothers for stealing his coat of many colors and then sell him to the Egyptians as a slave. Later alleged for a crime which he did not commit, he was cast into prison but by God's grace summoned to Pharaoh's court to interpret a dream which oblivious to him was the cause and effect for reuniting him with his brothers.

This alleged crime which landed him in prison is not only noteworthy in that it displayed the *character* of Joseph, which did not exist in most Biblical characters before and after him. One that was visibly embedded in the heart and soul of Jesus.

Joseph, even though he had forgiven his brothers for the injustice done to him, no doubt worked out extensively and toned up just in case he was ever placed in a situation where it was necessary for him to defend himself. He would be physically able to fight and win or his mere presence would be enough to intimidate any opponent.

Potiphar's wife must have seen him lifting heavy logs of wood in his spare time and doing pushups and realized how much he had bulked up growing excessive mass – muscle. To say the least, he was handsome in both form and appearance. She wanted him.

Joseph, on the other hand focusing on his job and character, even though she must have been a beautiful, drop dead gorgeous woman, he apparently paid little attention to her curves and package. This must have ticked her off. It's a given: when a woman knows that she's beautiful and powerful, dare a man not to at least notice her and tell her so. Her intuition certainly didn't reveal he wasn't *straight*. She wanted him and no doubt premeditated this upcoming ordeal.

One day while Potiphar was away she cunningly made her onslaught. "Come to bed with me." She said. Joseph apparently acted as if he didn't know what she was talking about. "Come and sleep with me." She demanded.

By this time, she, no doubt visualize Joseph caving in, possibly by making herself more appealing. "Lie with me." She continued. It's customary when lust supersedes, decency, reputation and conscience are all sacrificed. It's evident her heart was fully set on doing evil.

On the other hand, Satan realized he couldn't overcome Joseph with un-forgiveness and other troubles of the world, for in them he was resolute. So he had Potiphar's wife lay on the table what's most pleasurable to a man – sex. A vice which has proven to be the downfall of powerful men in the past, present and will be in the future.

In the meantime, Joseph was able to by the grace of God, resist and overcome this temptation. That same power of God which had been existent with Daniel in the lion's den, the three Hebrew boys in the fiery furnace, the Children of Israel crossing the Red Sea and the river of Jordan, as well as when Jesus performed multiple miracles was there at that moment for Joseph.

THE CHURCH...A HOSPITAL?

Imagine: Potiphar's wife rolls back the sliding doors and then the curtain which separated her bedroom from the living quarters. Before, she peeped at Joseph doing his chores. Now, Joseph and Potiphar's wife shares an open stage. She's adorned in her favorite negligee. In the backdrop, her bed is neatly made, dressed with her most costly bed linen.

At her request, sweet romantic music by her harpist obscured on the upper level resonates, while his favorite cologne evaporates from the bath tub. A bath towel large enough for Joseph next to a rag – hangs. A wood fire in the furnace burns cozily, while the gentle breeze aids the flickering light from a candle located on the bed stand. Finally, she lunges out and grabs Joseph.

Even so, Joseph considered: (1) Who he was that was being tempted. (2)What the sin was to which he had been tempted. (3)Against whom he had been tempted to sin. No doubt it was God's grace which kept Joseph from succumbing to this temptation. It was said: He fled from it, escaping for his life. Not only that, his coat was left in the hands of Potiphar's wife. *Joseph fled as a bird from the snare and as a roe from its hunter.* According to one writer.

Joseph understood genuine leadership. He was put in control of all that was in Potiphar's house. Except for the forbidden territory – his wife. He fled rather than indulging with that which doesn't belong to him.

THE CHURCH...A HOSPITAL?

In regards to trust. If a man can leave another man, in the presence of his wife without that man getting intimately involved with her, that man is not only trustworthy but a gentleman.

Potiphar's wife later lied to her husband concerning the incident and as a result, Joseph was cast into prison. However, God was with Joseph.

CHAPTER 8

There's an echo of Joseph's story which we must both hear and feel. When Potiphar came home and saw Joseph's coat, he was awestruck. His wife told him Joseph attacked her. She screamed. He ran away. Joseph's coat could probably be laying in the bed for Potiphar to see. No wonder when he heard the story he was outraged and put Joseph in prison.

THE CHURCH...A HOSPITAL?

We must note: Joseph was accounted for wearing two coats. The coat of many colors which his brothers confiscated before selling him into slavery and the other which he left in the hands of Potiphar's wife as he fled from her sexual scheme.

Joseph was willing to give up what made him feel warm and comfortable (those coats) in order to do the Lord's bidding.

Additionally, Joseph did not only shine when he landed in Egypt but as a kid while wearing that coat of many colors. No wonder his brothers envied him, sought to take his life and finally sold him into slavery. It is a fact that others tend to reject you when you shine too bright for them. No wonder Joseph became his brother's target and led to them confiscating his coat and sold him into slavery. They thought Joseph's shining ability was in his coat of many colors. However, they found out later Joseph's illumination was ingrained when they had no choice but to kneel before him years later when he was put in charge of distributing food when a serious famine in their land brought them face to face with him.

He also shone at Potiphar's house and when Potiphar's wife made her sexual advancement, he basically let her know she can have his coat but not his soul – he fled. Then she lied about the encounter.

Has anyone ever lied about you? How does it feel to be falsely accused especially by members of the same household of faith? "A lying tongue is an abomination to God."

We hear it whenever one's accused. We want Justice! Sometimes justice doesn't happen right away. However, it does happen. In Joseph's case, God had a better plan. As a script writer, if I was writing Joseph's story as an original account: In my follow-up scene, I would demand justice. I would probably invent a witness who overheard dialog between Potiphar's wife and Joseph. Maybe the harpist who played brilliantly. I would also have Potiphar to demand the truth from his wife by offering her rewards too good to pass up. In today's environment, I'll have some DNA evidence collected in order to support the case. When I found out Joseph was innocent, I would also demand him freed from prison.

However, we find God blessed everything Joseph did. It was so evident, the man who ran the prison couldn't help noticing. So as in the case like Potiphar's, the prison warden also put Joseph in charge. It was evident he shone in every job which he was assigned to. The Lord was with Joseph all the while he was imprisoned. Most of all it was noticeable. The light which shone on Joseph is still available today. However, we must understand with that light we become a magnet drawing antagonists as well as cooperatives. Sadly most cooperatives are transformed into antagonists as a result of our bright beams. They can't stand to see us shine.

THE CHURCH…A HOSPITAL?

That light returned and beamed in the Psalmists David after he cried out to be made whole.
"Where can I go from Your Spirit?
Or where can I flee from Your presence?
If I ascend into heaven, You are there;

If I make my bed in hell, behold, You are there.
If I take the wings of the morning,
And dwell in the uttermost parts of the sea,
Even there Your hand shall lead me,
And Your right hand shall hold me. (Psalms 139:7-10).

CHAPTER 9

In Old Testament time, David was classified as a man after God's own heart. Yet, he was caught in a downward spiral of sin. As we recount the story:

It was late one afternoon when David arose from his couch and went walking on the roof of the king's

THE CHURCH...A HOSPITAL?

house. He saw a woman bathing; she was very beautiful. David could not resist her beauty and sent and inquired about her. And one said, "Is not this Bathsheba, the daughter of Eliam, the wife of Uriah the Hittite? So David sent messengers and took her and she came to him, and he took her...Then she returned to her house. And the woman conceived, and she sent and told David, "I am pregnant."

David looking for a twist in the story and trying to cover up his sin and sought Uriah her husband from battle so Uriah could lie with her and think it was his baby. Uriah, on the other hand, was too noble to go into his wife while his comrades were engaged in battle. So David arranged to have him killed so he David could quickly marry Bathsheba and cover up the act of adultery.

It was said: "The thing that David did displeased the Lord" (2 Samuel 11:27). So God sent the prophet Nathan to David with a parable which entices David to pronounce his own condemnation. Nathan cleverly says: "You are the man!" and further asks, "Why have you despised the word of the Lord?" David breaks out into confession, "I have sinned against the Lord." Nathan replied astonishingly, "The Lord has put away your sin; you shall not die. Nevertheless, because by this deed you have utterly scorned the Lord, the child who is born to you shall die" (2 Samuel 12:7-15).

THE CHURCH...A HOSPITAL?

In this sequence of events: Bathsheba is raped. Uriah is dead. The Baby will die. Yet Nathan told David, "The Lord has put away your sin." Let's recount just in case you missed it. David committed adultery. He ordered the execution of Uriah. He also lied. Yet, the God stepped in and forgave him of those sins. David, forgiven for those sins is now made whole in the sight of God. Is this supernatural or is it supernatural? We are told in Psalms 51, David cried out to God:

Firstly, David turns to his only hope. "Have mercy upon me, O God, according to your steadfast love; according to your abundant mercy blot out my transgressions." We find here in Verse 1, mercy was solicited three times: *Have mercy, according to your steadfast love* and *according to your abundant mercy.*

Secondly, David prays for cleansing. Verse 2: "Wash me thoroughly from my iniquity, and cleanse me from my sin." Verse 7: Purge me with hyssop, and I shall be clean; wash me, and I shall be whiter than snow." Whiter than snow is a far cry by any stretch of one's imagination.

Thirdly, David confesses the seriousness of his sin possibly by counting all five fingers on his left hand while kneeling before God.

THE CHURCH…A HOSPITAL?

1. Verse 3: "For I know my transgressions, and my sin is ever before me."
2. Verse 4: "Against you, you only, have I sinned and done this evil in your sight."
3. Verse 4: …so that you may be justified in your words and blameless in your judgment."
4. Verse 5: "behold I was brought forth in iniquity, and in sin did my mother conceive me."
5. Verse 6: 'Behold, you delight in truth in the inward being, and you teach me wisdom in the secret heart."

David, you see had been a man after God's own heart but sin got the upper hand. Psalms 51 continues, with him pleading for renewal.

"A broken spirit and a contrite heart God will not despise."

You might be warming a seat somewhere in your church, holding a prestigious office. Maybe you have possession of the Church's keys. Maybe you dominate the conversation on the Church Board. Maybe you're the first one to voice scriptures whenever the opportunity presents itself. Maybe you lead out in song service with your melodious voice and commanding the highest note. Maybe you're adept at playing every instrument in the church and playing them *by air* you know every note of every song inside the church hymnal. Maybe you could recite the Bible from Genesis to Revelation. Maybe you're placed in position as the leader of the flock. Yet, you're spiraling down the pathway of inequity.

Are you ready for your spiritual check-up from the neck up? Are you ready to give up those secret sins which you alone can see in you?

Those sins of un-forgiveness, pride, doubt, covetousness, lust, malice, envy, strife, blasphemy, bigotry, vanity and witchcraft. All barriers, which prevent true intimacy with God.

As we recount the story of Achan in Joshua 7. It was because of hidden sins which resulted in the scheme to steal and hide what the Lord had commanded Israel not to touch. Achan disobeyed God and as a result he and his family suffered the consequences of Jericho and his inhabitants; for keeping part of Jericho which God said should be totally destroyed.

The truism screams: *Deeds done in darkness will eventually come to light.*

Jesus, the great Physician was so adept at reading the thoughts of many in his day. He still can today. What if he was to one day let others in on the secret sins which you harbor?

Just know that his grace is sufficient and he could pronounce you with a clean bill of health if you were to surrender your all to his will.

THE CHURCH…A HOSPITAL?

Let's visit our local church as this chronicle unfolds in the lives of some of its members. Brace yourself as we journey together.

CHAPTER 10

The mantra echoing in Christendom today is a relationship. To put this in proper perspective: A genuine relationship. The key word being *genuine*. We either have a genuine relationship with Jesus Christ or we're working towards one. There should be no in-betweens. Some members, are simply prepared to warm the pews or on a more premeditated non-productive level – play Church.

The people who play church are the bystanders who sits next to you and me in church, who give us their half-hearted worship and appreciation or disinfect their hands right after shaking yours or several during a meet and greet "Smile awhile." They seem to know everything going on in the lives of the other members while theirs is worse than a cesspool. "Look what she wore today. That same pair of shoes which matches everything inside her wardrobe. Why can't she get herself a husband instead of talking with those who are already married or the men who are already involved in a relationship?

Why is she always the first to show up for everything and the last to leave? Why does the pastor always seem to favor her? Why is she always favored? Where did she find that cheap winter coat? She must have purchased it from the thrift store." And on and on. Everybody's business is their business.

The Church's business is very low on their agenda if at all. They allow their kids to run their homes. Therefore, when those kids show up at church, no one dares suggest anything having to do with their proper attitude in and around the facility. They run wild without a leash. "Do not address my child." They would say, complainingly. If they don't like what is said during the service they are not hesitant to voice their differences of opinion.

THE CHURCH...A HOSPITAL?

When it's time to evangelize, they don't want to have anything to do with it. However, when you bring someone new to the church and they accept the Lord as their personal Savior. They are first in line to tell them everything that's wrong with the church and everyone else including you. They know how many times a month you put your tithes and offering in the basket. Whenever you throw in loose offering they even know the dollar amount. They hear everything wrong. They see everything wrong. They know everything's wrong. They gossip and slander as if it's going out of style. Their Bible, which contains a five-chapter book known as The General Epistle of James does nothing for them but accumulate dust.

Their negative actions of yesterday paint a blurry, pixelated picture of their tomorrow. They advance spiritually with one foot forward and two feet backward. Every day they vow they will turn their life around and never does. The light which once shone brightly within them has extinguished. The have a form of Godliness but deny the power thereof. They speak so loudly, yet you can't hear what they say much less see it displayed.

Welcome to the world of *they* sitting right next to you and me inside the church. Sometimes right on the front pew.

AS YOU READ ON, some stories will not only stir up in you a desire to walk closer with God but have you examine that hike closely. Don't be surprised if the question: *How do I stack up with God as well as my fellowmen?* haunts you.

Some names have been changed in order to protect the identity of those individuals.

CHAPTER 11

Many of us live our lives, saying one thing and then doing the complete opposite. We aren't careful to stick to what we've said we have agreed to do. It seems as if dyslexia steps in as soon as we close our mouths. The words we say from our mouths tend not to be close or near what we purpose in our minds. Our *yeah* and our *no* has flipped. Therefore like clockwork we've rewritten the script.

Hypocrisy has become a comfortable flaw in the lives of many endeavoring to walk the Christian pathway. It is defined as a feigning to be what one is not or to believe what one does not; *especially*: the false assumption of an appearance of virtue or religion. Synonyms which describe Hypocrisy are insecurity, two-faced-ness, pretense, double-standards, and duplicity. The antonym of Hypocrisy is security.

The number of times Jesus condemned Hypocrisy far outweighs all other sins. It is evident that he saw much hypocrisy than anything else in the people of his day. He repeatedly condemned those teachers of the law and the Pharisees for their hypocritical practices. *Matthew 23* tells that story. He also instructs us not to criticize others when we have housed habits worse than theirs. The truism screams: Whenever we point one finger at someone else we have three of our own fingers pointing back at us.

In Jesus' tenancy here on earth, he told numerous stories. It was said: He spoke in parables at least forty-six instances. Mainly, so that even the uneducated could *catch his drift*. One writer states: *A parable is a story or an illustration placed alongside a truth with the intention of explaining one by the other.* Additionally, the early definition of a parable says *It's an earthly story with a heavenly meaning, some familiar thing of life on earth placed alongside some mystery of heaven, that our understanding of the one may help us understand the other.*

On this particular instance, Jesus referred to the mote in our brother's eye. *Thou hypocrite, first cast out the beam out of thine own eye; and then shalt thou see clearly to cast out the mote out of thy brother's eye:* According to Matthew 7:5 KJV. Jesus used much colorful imaginary and wit while ridiculing the religious leaders of his day. There's no doubt he wanted the picture to remain vividly with them. Matthew 23:27-28 (KJV) *Woe unto you, scribes and Pharisees, hypocrites! for ye are like unto whited sepulchers, which indeed appear beautiful outward, but are within full of dead men's bones, and of all uncleanness. Even so ye also outwardly appear righteous unto men, but within ye are full of hypocrisy and iniquity.* Ouch! They looked pretty on the outside. However, on the inside, they were a mess or equated to *dead men's bones.*

CHAPTER 12

D aniel and Priscilla Harris, now entering mid-life grew up in the local church. The church building dedicated almost 50 years ago is a landmark in the New York City neighborhood. They were just a few years shy of witnessing the laying of its huge granite cornerstone.

Daniel had the hearts for Priscilla since both of them functioned in the AY department. She singing her heart out as a chorister and him, the leader in an all-male quartet.

The two tied the knot years later as they reached their mid-twenties. Years later, they were not only blessed with three children, two boys, and one girl but multiple church offices accompanied their rise to popularity within the organization. Soon their burn out became noticeable both in church duties and each other.

It wasn't long afterward, Daniel stopped attending church. It seems as though he had enough. He even found a job on the Sabbath so he wouldn't attend.

Priscilla, on the other hand, continued shuffling her feet, and it wasn't long before she began skipping church along with her kids, now teenagers.

Multiple calls were placed to Daniel, mainly by two elders of the church, Petersen, and Reid regarding his absence. Daniel cleverly dodged their calls and some he never returned.

Finally, Priscilla got tired of being avoided. As other members avoided her, including Sister Bev and Sister Grace who headed up the welcome committee. Many passed her by during the welcome song as if she had leprosy or the plague. Even though the young pastor at the time spoke consistently concerning hypocrisy and loving others as you love yourself, it didn't matter to most members who warmed the church's pews.

To make matters worse, when Priscilla got home she told Daniel everything that went wrong during that

THE CHURCH…A HOSPITAL?

church visit. "They are just a bunch of hypocrites!" Daniel echoed. On the inside, her husband had now been harboring strong resentment for the church as well as everything it stood for. One night a heated debate erupted concerning what was wrong with the church along with all those phone calls made in an attempt to woe Daniel back to the fold.

It was evident by now, Daniel had other plans as he packed all of those Ellen G. White books sitting in their book library inside a box and sealed it with tape. Obviously, those books reminded him of who he had become and still can evolve into. The library shelves now became home to his favorite pop artists.

Meanwhile, the house once filled with morning and evening devotion was littered with arguments and disrespect. Daniel not only stayed out late but treated Priscilla as if she was a foreign object.

CHAPTER 13

On his way to work one day, Daniel lost control of the car's steering wheel and ran over an embankment. *The car rolled multiple times,* according to one eyewitness. Luckily, he only incurred two broken legs. As a result, he was geared with crutches. The following Sabbath he wobbled through the church doors on props with his family following in tow.

THE CHURCH...A HOSPITAL?

Sister Bev and Grace greets them at the door with a half-hearted "Great to see you back." As the Harris family went through the doors and into the sanctuary, the welcoming sisters continue on their fault finding pursuit. Most of the seats were taken. However, the front row was vacant. So the Harris family occupy.

Across the way, Petersen and Reid huddles. "You see brother Harris. He finally returned to church but now he's on two crutches." Says Elder Petersen.

"Yes, I see him. I don't know why he thinks he can run from God. Every time I called him he said he'll get back with me and never did. You cannot hide from God."

"I know, he cannot run now what made him think he could hide. Look at him, now he is sitting on those prime seats in the front row. He never sent us any offerings to buy those pews. Those seats belong to Sister Smith, dead and gone home to meet Jesus. She's the one who took out a second mortgage on her house so we could have those seats. Brother Harris threw in the towel and bought that fancy automobile right when we were in the red. Now that thing almost cost him his life."

One of the Deacons came by and engaged Elder Petersen. Elder Reid on the other hand, left, thereby aborting the conversation.

Meanwhile, within the congregation, two Sisters: one seated on the second row and the other on the last row to the back are busily involved – texting each other. They pay no attention to the message being preached by their pastor – Pastor Epps. In addition to their text-ability, they glance at the Harris' periodically.

Some members cast looks of annoyance while cluing in regarding their false sense of worship or what one may call irreverence.

Even so, others are focused on hearing the Word delivered.

CHAPTER **14**

A t the end of the service, many greeted the
Harris family with their "Good to see you."
One of them included the Church Clerk,
Sister Rogers, an elderly woman with the demeanor of
a Patriarch.

"It's great to see you. We heard about your tragedy.
What can we do to help?" With pride swelling up in

their hearts the members of the Harris family made no request of Sister Rogers.

With most of the congregation cleared out, the family seemed glued to that front row as if waiting for their diagnosis from the Great Physician.

The song of surrender resonates in Daniel's heart, soul, and mind. Suddenly, a voice echoes: "Daniel, you know that woman you've been seeing for the last two years. She's pregnant with child and is desperately considering an abortion. Tell her not to do it." Daniel looks across at his wife and kids, with a look of embarrassment. However, they were oblivious to the message as it was only intended for Daniel.

The voice continues: "Daniel, one of the books you've packed away inside that box is the Bible, the Holy Word. I need for you to open the box, dust the Bible off and start reading it again, more than you've done on previous occasions. Begin with the verse (John 11:35) "Jesus wept." Daniel Harris enables his two crutches and makes his way through the exit.

The voice continues "Priscilla, let go of your boss. His wife needs him. Stop engaging in malice, envy, and strife. They are the works of the Devil. Plus, the money which you transferred from your husband's account yesterday. You need to return it. If you take it to Las Vegas you are going to blow all of it."

Priscilla attempts to get up but sits back down with the three kids.

THE CHURCH…A HOSPITAL?

The voice continues: "Children, obey your parents in the Lord: for this is right. (Ephesians 6:1).

The three Harris' kids turn and look at each other as the message speaks to them.

The voice continues:

"Honor your father and mother"--which is the first commandment with a promise — "(Ephesians 6:2).

They exit the sanctuary, rush past Sister Bev and Sister Grace, still engrossed in their conversation and join their mom and dad in tears, as they make their exit of the Church.

IN REALITY, smart people do dumb things. Wise people and even Godly people do dumb, sinful things. Regardless of how we all messed up, we can still recover. "…all have sinned and fall short of the glory of God. (Romans 3:23). Even so, we can all rebound and score that victory in Jesus.

Coming clean with God requires honesty. Sometimes we are not only afraid of losing our reputation of being publicly exposed that we are afraid of losing the security we got from indulging in our favorite sin. However, the peace we attain from coming clean with God is invaluable. With God, we never lose.

As we ask for forgiveness, as in the case of David, Peter, and many others including the Harris' family. His cleansing power is adequate to make us clean again. The pitfall occurs when we are not willing to own our mistakes along with its consequences. David cried out: "For I know my transgressions, and my sin is always before me."

God's forgiveness is always available to us. Even so, in order to experience it, we first need to believe we are forgiven, accepted and loved unconditionally.

Walking away from sin is a giant step in our Christian walk. Later in this book, we'll discuss the benefits of doing so.

CHAPTER 15

On that day, the return of the Harris' family not only lingered on the minds of elder's Petersen and Reid but on the minds of others as well. The Harris family had left the building. However, their gossip and backbiting continued.

"Death and life are in the power of the tongue: and they that love it shall eat the fruit thereof," (Proverbs

THE CHURCH…A HOSPITAL?

18:31). "Let no corrupt communication proceed out of your mouth, but that which is good to the use of edifying, that it may minister grace unto the hearers." According to Ephesians 4:29. And James 1:26 supports: "If any man among you seem to be religious, and bridleth not his tongue, but deceiveth his own heart, this man's religion is in vain." One would think that in such a leadership role in the Church, these two elders would bridle their tongue. Yet, at the lunch table, they sat together and continued their spew of negatives regarding Brother Harris and family.

Suddenly, that same voice echoes and only to the hearing of elder Peterson's ears. "James Petersen! You take delight in tearing others apart. Where's your ability of discipleship?" The voice gets his attention. Elder Reid continues speaking but Petersen hears nothing he says. That voice continues: "Will a man rob God? Yet ye have robbed me. But ye say, Wherein have we robbed thee? In tithes and offerings." Elder Petersen looks across at the now quiet elder Reid to see if he's eavesdropping on the conversation. The voice continues: "You pay your tithes with irregularity. You give a very little offering. Remember Ananias and Sapphira? They withheld what belonged to the Lord. Reread their account in Acts chapter 4."

Elder Petersen could not believe his own ears. Still, the voice continues: "A wholesome tongue is a tree of life: but perverseness therein is a breach in the spirit."

THE CHURCH...A HOSPITAL?

(Proverbs 15:14). "But the tongue can no man tame; it is an unruly evil, full of deadly poison." (James 3:8). Suddenly, a song of consecration burns on the lips of Elder Petersen. Elder Reid, not knowing what has transpired in those moments leading up, excuses himself from the lunch table.

CHAPTER **16**

During service the following week, the Church Clerk announced that Sister Bev has been diagnosed with terminal cancer and is awaiting the doctor's decision whether or not to undergo chemotherapy.

Meanwhile, Sister Bev at home, besides changing her diet to wheat grass and other herbs, was spending

THE CHURCH…A HOSPITAL?

much time on her knees with God. She had also etched some of her favorite one-liners on index cards and kept repeating them to herself. She paced around her house, looking through the window as if her healing was somewhere outside while repeating her affirmations.

- No weapon formed against me shall prosper.

- "I can do all things through Christ which strengtheneth me." (Phil. 4:13 KJV)

- "The steps of a good *woman* are ordered by the Lord." (Ps. 37:23 KJV)

- I refuse to renounce my self-image, no matter what happens to me.

- The battle is not mine; it belongs to the Lord.

- What God has for me no devil in hell can take.

- I was born to fight this.

- The time has come for my change.

- God is taking me where no woman has gone before.

- I must beat cancer.

- I can have what God says I can have.

- I will arise! I will finish.

THE CHURCH...A HOSPITAL?

- When it's all said and done, I'll come out of it.

- I'm the head and not the tail.

- You may whip some but not me. I'm going to force you to give up.

- I have what it takes to fight cancer.

- I'm a giant killer.

- I'm chosen. I can take less and do more with it.

- God wants me to be so blessed that I live in the land of much.

- God is opening doors for me that no one can shut.

Immediately after those positive affirmations, she took a sip of her wheatgrass and erupts in song. Suddenly, the voice permeates: "But I say unto you, that every word that man shall speak, they shall give account thereof in the judgment." (Matthew 13:36-37).
Sister Bev looks aggravated.
The voice continues: "The heart of the righteous studieth to answer: but the mouth of the wicked pour out evil things." (Proverbs 15:28).
There is silence as Sister Bev seeks for more clarity from the voice. There's nothing.

THE CHURCH…A HOSPITAL?

She gets up from her seat on the couch where she planted herself in order to take in whatever the voice ushered. "Finally …whatsoever things are honest, whatsoever things are just, whatsoever things are pure, whatsoever things are lovely, whatsoever things are of good report; if there be any virtue and if there be any praise, think on these things." (Philippians 4:8).

The voice fades.

Sister Bev resonates and erupts in song…

CHAPTER **17**

Weeks later, Sister Bev returned to her local Church. She was not only happy being in fellowship once again but her doctor who previously gave her a few weeks to live (after a recent diagnosis) informed her that she was cancer free.

When she walked through the doors of the Church, how her face shone with brightness, her chest stuck out, and her head held high. Sister Bev walked with a feeling of confidence. Not only knowing she had been healed of what is usually termed a fatal disease but she had cleaned up her act and in search of fullness in Jesus Christ.

Sister Grace was not at the welcoming location that morning, neither was she anywhere within the congregation. Sister Bev had purposed in her heart not only to share the good news of her encounter with the Great Physician. He had not only washed her sins away and made her clean again but had miraculously cured her of the deadly disease - cancer.

Sister Bev, with tears in her eyes, gave her testimony that day in Church. She not only mentioned about her cure but how for so long she had been engaged in gossip, slander as well as hypocrisy. She further asked if there's anyone who she had wronged knowingly or unknowingly to be forgiven by that brother or sister. She carried a song in her heart and on her lips. plus a total transformation in her attitude. As she hummed, one could not only sense her conviction but her conversion and commitment as well.

The service ended and Sister Bev embraced anyone and everyone in her path. How the now healed sister, wished she had done that prior as she officiated on the Welcome Team. How she wished she had been a genuine Greeter, filled with the love of Jesus and for her fellowmen. Many, who she negatively turned

THE CHURCH...A HOSPITAL?

away could have decided never to return because someone gave them the cold shoulder – Sister Bev.

How many times do we miss the opportunity to have someone feel much better about themselves after they've left us? It is said: "We only have one chance to make a first impression." Is that encounter one we are proud of? Is it a door opener to soul winning or an aid toward cementing one's belief in our Great Physician? Or like Sister Bev, who for so long hid behind those sins of the mind and heart?

Thankfully, she was given the opportunity to come to grips with herself and turn her life around. Some never heal from such diseases of mind and body.

CHAPTER 18

W hile Sister Bev was making her exit from the Church lobby. She visually connected with Sister Grace, who just entered. It wasn't long before they were in each other's arms. It had become News to Sister Grace, that Sister Bev had been cured of cancer and returned to Church that day. Grace who had backslid or what some might call "On

THE CHURCH...A HOSPITAL?

Sabbatical" since Sister Bev got sick. She had lost the presence of her Gossip Buddy (GB).

Sister Harris, who had been slandered by both Sisters Bev and Grace was present to greet Sister Bev when she walked through the doors that morning. Soon after Sister Harris texted Sister Grace breaking the good news regarding Sister Bev's healing and return to Church.

AT HOME, Sister Grace, relaxing on her couch and watching TV, received that text hurried, and made it there just in time to see her GB just before she exited the facility. Sister Grace made it her duty to dump whatever gossip she thought she kept reserved on Sister Bev. However, Sister Bev would have none of it. It suddenly became clear to Sister Grace that her GB was not only cured of cancer but she was also cured of gossip and all of the gossip's affiliates. In case there was any doubt as to where she stood, Sister Bev went Bible on her. "Doth a fountain send forth at the same place sweet water and bitter? Can the fig tree, my brethren, bear olive berries? Either a vine, figs? So can no fountain yield salt water and fresh?

Who is a wise man and endued with knowledge among you? Let him shew out of good conversation his works with meekness of wisdom." (James 3:11-13).

Sister Grace somewhat dumbfounded found herself in a daze. The same voice which had spoken now on multiple occasions uttered solely to her:

THE CHURCH...A HOSPITAL?

"But if you have bitter envy in your hearts, glory not, and lie not against the truth.

For where envy and strife is, there is confusion and every evil work." (James 3: 14 & 16).

Something had resonated inside Sister Grace's heart and mind. She immediately began worshipping in song while in the presence of Sister Bev. It was so melodious many came and joined in, including the Harris' family.

CHAPTER 19

We find Elder Reid on the tailspin of his two-year term in office as the first elder of the local Church. His desire when he was elected was to take the church's evangelism effort to new unreachable heights. Instead, he lost hope, on multiple occasion he disagreed with and confronted the Church's pastor. He at one point confided in Elder

THE CHURCH...A HOSPITAL?

Petersen, the second elder. Collectively they had heard how both elders had filled the church with bigotry and slander. Even so, elder Petersen had cleaned up his life and we find elder Reid heading on a spiritual downward spiral.

With the Church elections ongoing, Reid decided he had enough and sent a letter to the Church Board. In it, he explained his grievances and called it quit. Not only was the worship mood a somber one but most members not only spread the news of his resignation like wildfire, they distributed their negative attitude about the pastor to anyone who would listen.

It was rumored, Elder Reid and the Pastor were mismanaging the church's finances. Those close to the pastor prayed earnestly to stop the runaway train of slander.

However, the news was moving so fast many dashed out of the way. It was evident someone on the church board had been leaking information to the body of the church. How did it for some time now remained a mystery.

The election ended. A new first elder was voted in – Elder Petersen. So now one slandering brother was out and the other who had cleaned up his life was in. Now elder Reid because of character issues was unable to pass the baton.

Slander kept its reins on him and he could not shake it loose. It is said about a HABIT. If you remove the H you still have ABIT. If you remove the A you still have BIT. And if you remove the B you still have IT.

CHAPTER 20

Some members saw it a progressive move to elect Petersen as the first elder. Others who had been on the receiving end of his slander in the past not only displayed antagonism toward him on the inside but like anything when it has too much it is sure to explode. They had experienced the backlash of him and Reid and were not ready to forgive either. Some

THE CHURCH...A HOSPITAL?

felt it was not only a friendship but church politics which move Petersen into the church top office. Some felt it was not Holy Ghost directed. Some felt Petersen had not given up his slandering and feared the worse was about to happen.

On the other hand, many wished Reid had cleaned up his act because he seemed like the better choice if he did. Still they felt the church pastor was in the wrong end of it all. "After all, he's the leader of the flock." They complained. Church services continued but on a low ebb. The hymns dragged, lacking sweet flames as well as inspiration.

As these services declined in spirituality, elder Reid didn't have problems drawing a crowd wherever he was on church property. The lobby being his most used space. Many wanted to hear from him firsthand. The news of the day along with church politics, who was effective in their church duties, who paid tithes and offerings. If you wanted to know just ask elder Reid. He was like the Church's statistician. Seasoned church members not only flocked the lobby during service but new converts, youths and even tiny tots accompanied by their parents. Whatever elder Reid had to say seems like it took precedent over what was being delivered from the pulpit.

The business of the church board continued to leak out to the body by Reid. It was a mystery how he got access to such classified information. Sister Grace was now sitting on the board and it was learned she was using

THE CHURCH...A HOSPITAL?

her smartphone extensively during the meetings. Another board member decided to eavesdrop on her texting and realized she was texting to Reid during the board meetings.

She informed him regarding what was voted on and not. Even the meeting's minutes she shared with him. It is said you can take a pig out of mud but you can't take mud out of a pig. Sister Grace was still up to mischief within the church.

The milieu was not only sick but like one stricken with stage four cancer – death was eminent.

CHAPTER 21

I t was another Wednesday night prayer meeting at the local church. Elder Petersen seized the opportunity to bear his testimony. It was more of a confession rather than giving thanks. It so happened more members were in attendance on that particular night that there had ever been in a long time. He proceeded to cite David's sin which led to the killing of Uriah.

THE CHURCH...A HOSPITAL?

Most members in attendance knew he had engaged in slander for a long time and more so when The Harris' Family were going through their situations and wrestling with God. Some forgave elder Petersen while many did not.

He continued: ... "Lord, I was wrong. You said in your word to love one another as you've loved me. Yet, I've despised others. Called them names. Lied about their situations. I did not let brotherly love flow. Worse of all, I did not entertain strangers. I'm sorry if those angels disappeared because of me." Elder Petersen began humming a song as he rose from his knees and took it to higher heights.

Many in the room that night not only joined in but rose their voices mightily in *I surrender all.* The aura was short of nothing but a Hallelujah breakdown.

The song ended and many huddled around elder Petersen. Sister Petersen broke down in tears as the huddle expanded as hands waited their turn to shake that of their first elder. The organist found something he could play and latch onto it. More and more members left their seats and joined the crowd in unison.

It seemed as if many had now left their worries behind them and with sympathy and empathy latched onto the evolving breaking down of their first elder. Even the half a dozen youths, there with their parents were now out of their seats and rendering the lyrics to the instrumental musical rendition from the organist.

THE CHURCH...A HOSPITAL?

As the song continued, a few walk-ins had heard it. It seemed to have done their heart some good. They, even though dressed in their street clothes had entered the church lobby and joined in the singing.

CHAPTER 22

It was evident the church wasn't growing. Many sensed there was a leadership problem. Yet, many made no attempt to fix it. Like a runaway, train stopping seemed to be nothing but a collision or even worse a derailment until elder Petersen found a way to apply the brakes. He as well as others praised in their church office and only did enough for their own glory instead of being all they can be in order to move God's church forward.

Bad people or what you may classify *sick members* at this local church had consistently ran things and other members were groaning. Was this the fix needed by the church or this was just a band-aid applied to stop the bleeding and cover up the injury?

It is said, a stitch in time saves nine. There was no effort made earlier even if the handwriting was on the wall. As it turned out that train kept running and Pastor Epps incurred the blame. As a result, his replacement was imminent. Meetings were held by the conference which oversees in order to determine who would stop the runaway church from calamity taking a congregation of over 200 members down a path of no return.

In the meantime, church members groaned and complained. How they would have liked to make that decision for themselves. Yet, the Conference was the one in charge of calling those shots.

Soon the news surfaced. Pastor Epps' replacement was in question. Pastor Bailey, the incumbent was easy going. However, he was a man from the streets of New York. It was not only apparent he had seen and witnessed the affairs of the streets but he had an affinity with the drums. As a previous Master Guide leader, he had trained many the art of the Drumline. He loved a little *ooh* and *aah* in his music especially on

THE CHURCH…A HOSPITAL?

Sabbath mornings just before the praise team did their multiple hymns rendition.

The local congregation not only heard about his disciplinary skills but his worship style as well. This did not sit well with elder Reid nor his newly formed clique. To say the least, they had previously revolted in their minds and now it was being acted out in their mannerisms. Contrary to Pastor Epps' wishes, who was now on his way out: meetings on Sabbaths was a big No-No. Meetings were held by various newly formed cliques to determine if the new pastor should be accepted or not.

CHAPTER 23

It was decided in a meeting held by one of the larger cliques that Pastor Bailey wasn't welcomed if a drum set was going to accompany him to this new appointment as the leader of the flock. Many of its members were not only seasoned but had been the founding mothers and fathers. Some of them held and witnessed the laying of the building's cornerstone. The

THE CHURCH...A HOSPITAL?

investment in the multiple layers of carpeting before and now was part of their savings. The pulpit and the chandelier were of their giving as well as the pews, the chairs, the organ, the sound system as well as the baptismal fount.

Nowhere were they prepared to have a drum set change or alter their customs of worship. The Conferences' decision was final as the governing body of the church and Pastor Bailey's arrival was less than a week away.

WHEN THE DOORS OPENED that following Sabbath morning, not only the sound system was missing, the song service leader and several other church leaders were missing from that congregation.

Meanwhile, almost one mile away, elder Reid, Sister Grace, and others were singing lustily the praises of their new *split*.

Instead of growing their local church until it burst through its seams with an overflow of members, and then divide up and conquer for the Lord, they had fallen into the epiphany of a premature and feuded split of their congregation. Not only that, they still debated and contested for items belonging to that church.

To make matters worse, the handful of young people who attended that church stayed envisioning the arrival of the drum set with broken hearts and trepidation. However, they were not heartily singing the praises of the breakup.

The Voice which had spoken to Brother Harris and his family, to Sister Bev, Sister Grace, elders Reid and Petersen returned and addressing each one at once including the new split but in privacy: "The kingdom of heaven is likened unto a man which sowed good seed in his field:

But while men slept, his enemy came and sowed tares among the wheat, and went his way."

The tares were sowed among the wheat and while growing the tares also look like wheat.

"But when the blade was sprung up, and brought forth fruit, then appeared the tares also."

Wheat is golden but the tares show their true color as they ripen. When the tares are full grown, the ears are long and the grains almost black. All the tares must be removed before grinding the wheat because they are poisonous.

"So the servants of the householder came and said unto him, Sir, didst not thou sow good seed in thy field? from whence then hath it tares?

He said unto them, An enemy hath done this. The servants said unto him, Wilt thou then that we go and gather them up?   But he said, Nay; lest while ye gather up the tares, ye root up also the wheat with them.

Let both grow together until the harvest: and in the time of harvest I will say to the reapers, Gather ye together first the tares, and bind them in bundles to burn them: but gather the wheat into my barn."

THE CHURCH...A HOSPITAL?

The voice ceased in both congregations simultaneously. Suddenly, Pastor Bailey begins humming a tune. A blind man makes his way into the sanctuary. The blind man began singing and held a tune like no other as he navigated his way to the front and joined in with the now singing Pastor Bailey... *I'll see all my friends in Hallelujah Square...* Many of the handicapped within that congregation also echoed in song. The Harris family left their seats and joined in singing tumultuously. The unused drum set as a display is next to the organ. However, it gets very little attention as more and more voices join and echo the words of *Hallelujah Square.*

About The Author

John A. Andrews hails from the beautiful Islands of St. Vincent and the Grenadines and resides in Hollywood, California. He is best known for his gritty and twisted writing style in his National Bestselling novel - Rude Buay ... The Unstoppable. He is in (2012) releasing this

THE CHURCH...A HOSPITAL?

chronicle in the French edition and poised to release its sequel Rude Buay ... The Untouchable in March 2012.

Andrews moved from New York to Hollywood in 1996, to pursue his acting career. With early success, he excelled as a commercial actor. Then tragedy struck - a divorce, with Andrews, granted joint custody of his three sons, Jonathan, Jefferri, and Jamison, all under the age of five. That dream of becoming all he could be in the entertainment industry now took on nightmarish qualities.

In 2002, after avoiding bankruptcy and a twisted relationship at his modeling agency, he fell in love with a 1970s classic film, which he wanted to remake. Subsequent to locating the studio which held those rights, his request was denied. As a result, Andrews decided that he was going to write his own. Not knowing how to write and failing constantly at it, he inevitably recorded his first bestseller, Rude Buay ... The Unstoppable in 2010: a drug prevention chronicle, sending a strong message to teens and adults alike

Andrews is also a visionary, and a prolific author who has etched over two dozen titles including: Dare to Make a Difference - Success 101 for Teens, The 5 Steps To Changing Your Life, Spread Some Love - Relationships 101, Quotes Unlimited, How I Wrote 8 Books in One Year, The FIVE "Ps" for Teens, Total

THE CHURCH...A HOSPITAL?

Commitment - The Mindset of Champions, and Whose Woman Was She? - A True Hollywood Story.

In 2007, Mr. Andrews a struggling actor and author etched his first book The 5 Steps to Changing Your Life. That title having much to do with changing one's thoughts, words, actions, character and changing the world. A book which he claims shaped his life as an author with now over two dozen published titles.

Andrews followed up his debut title with Spread Some Love - Relationships 101 in 2008, a title which he later turned into a one-hour docu-drama.

Additionally, during that year, Andrews wrote eight titles, including Total Commitment - The Mindset of Champions, Dare to Make A Difference - Success 101 for Teens, Spread Some Love - Relationships 101 (Workbook) and Quotes Unlimited.

After those publications in 2009, Andrews recorded his hit novel as well as Whose Woman Was She? and When the Dust Settles - I am Still Standing: his True Hollywood Story, now also being turned into a film.

New titles in the Personal Development genre include Quotes Unlimited Vol. II, The FIVE "Ps" For Teens, Dare to Make A Difference - Success 101 and Dare to Make A Difference - Success 101 - The Teacher's Guide.

THE CHURCH...A HOSPITAL?

His new translated titles include Chico Rudo ... El Imparable, Cuya Mujer Fue Ella? and Rude Buay ... The Unstoppable in Chinese.

Back in 2009, while writing the introduction of his debut book for teens: Dare To Make A Difference - Success 101 for Teens, Andrews visited the local bookstore. He discovered only 5 books in the Personal Development genre for teens while noticing hundreds of the same genre in the adult section. Sensing there was a lack of personal growth resources, focusing on youth 13-21, he published his teen book and soon thereafter founded Teen Success.

This organization is empowerment based, designed to empower Teens in maximizing their full potential to be successful and contributing citizens in the world.
Andrews referred to as the man with "the golden voice" is a sought after speaker on "Success" targeting young adults. He recently addressed teens in New York, Los Angeles, Hawaii and was the guest speaker at the 2011 Dr. Martin Luther King Jr. birthday celebrations in Eugene, Oregon.

John Andrews came from a home of educators; all five of his sisters taught school - two acquiring the status of school principals. Though self-educated, he understands the benefits of a great education and being all he can be. Two of his teenage sons are also writers. John spends most of his time writing, publishing books and traveling the country going on book tours.

Additionally, John Andrews is a screenwriter and producer and is in (2012) turning his bestselling novel into a film.

See more in:

HOW I RAISED MYSELF FROM FAILURE TO

SUCCESS IN HOLLYWOOD.

Visit: www.JohnAAndrews.com

Check out Upcoming Titles & New Releases...

HOW I RAISED MYSELF FROM FAILURE TO SUCCESS IN HOLLYWOOD

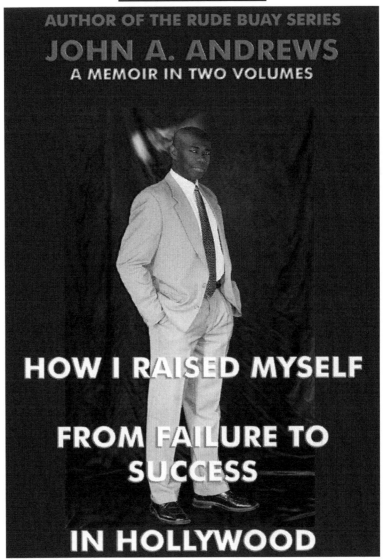

AUTHOR OF THE RUDE BUAY SERIES

JOHN A. ANDREWS

A MEMOIR IN TWO VOLUMES

HOW I RAISED MYSELF

FROM FAILURE TO SUCCESS

IN HOLLYWOOD

HOW I WROTE 8 BOOKS IN ONE YEAR

ANDREWS

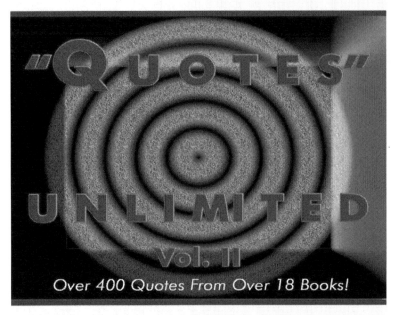

"QUOTES"

UNLIMITED

Vol. II

Over 400 Quotes From Over 18 Books!

John A. Andrews

National Bestselling Author of

RUDE BUAY ... THE UNSTOPPABLE

DARE TO MAKE A DIFFERENCE – SUCCESS 101

National Bestselling Author

Dare To Make A Difference

SUCCESS 101

JOHN A. ANDREWS

QUOTES UNLIMITED

THE 5 STEPS TO CHANGING YOUR LIFE

National Bestselling Author of
Rude Buay … The Unstoppable

THE 5
STEPS TO
CHANGING
YOUR LIFE
BY: JOHN A. ANDREWS

THE CHURCH...A HOSPITAL?

WHEN THE DUST SETTLES
I'M STILL STANDING

DARE TO MAKE A DIFFERENCE -
SUCCESS 101 FOR TEENS

THE 5 Ps FOR TEENS

THE CHURCH…A HOSPITAL?

SPREAD SOME LOVE – RELATIONSHIPS 101

THE CHURCH…A HOSPITAL?

TOTAL COMMITMENT

By National Bestselling Author of Rude Buay ... The Unstoppable

TOTAL COMMITMENT

The Mindset of Champions

JOHN A. ANDREWS

THE CHURCH…A HOSPITAL?

VISIT: WWW.JOHNAANDREWS.COM

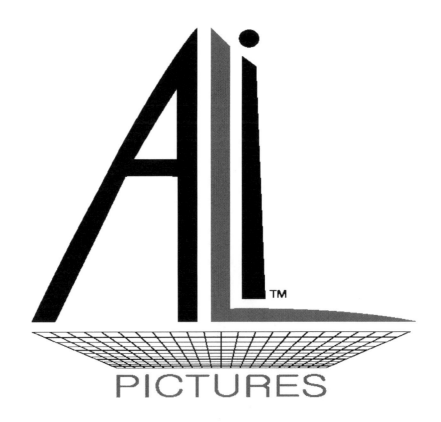

Optioned for A Musical Stage Play by:
A L I Pictures, LLC.

THE CHURCH…A HOSPITAL?

Unless otherwise indicated in the text, all Bible references used are from various versions of the Bible.

LIKE Us on FaceBook

https://www.facebook.com/JohnAAndrewsWritings/

THE CHURCH…A HOSPITAL?

NOTES

THE CHURCH…A HOSPITAL?

NOTES

THE CHURCH…A HOSPITAL?

<u>NOTES</u>

NOTES

NOTES

<u>NOTES</u>

NOTES

THE CHURCH…A HOSPITAL?

NOTES

NOTES

Made in the USA
Middletown, DE
07 February 2023

23465481R00073